ALIEN ABDUCTIONS

ENDURING MYSTERIES

KEN KARST

Published by
CREATIVE EDUCATION and CREATIVE PAPERBACKS

P.O. Box 227, Mankato, Minnesota 56002
Creative Education and Creative Paperbacks are imprints of The Creative Company
www.thecreativecompany.us

Design by Danny Nanos of Gilbert & Nanos
Production by Joe Kahnke
Art direction by Rita Marshall
Printed in China

Photographs by Alamy (Chronicle, RGR Collection), Creative Commons Wikimedia (Abestrobi, Carol Rainey, Gage Skidmore, Edward Valigursky/Amazing Stories), Dreamstime (Melkor3d), Getty Images (Colin Anderson/Blend Images, Glasshouse Images/Corbis, Bruce Hershey/Photolibrary, Hulton Archive/Stringer/Archive Photos, Keystone-France/ Gamma-Keystone, Science Picture Co), iStockphoto (jallfree, Neutronman, sakkmesterke, SSSCCC, titaniumdoughnut, Yuri_Arcurs), Newscom (Chris Clor Blend Images), Shutterstock (adike, Andrii_M, Leo Blanchette, byvalet, CLIPAREA/Custom media, andrea crisante, diversepixel, Dotted Yeti, JoeFotoSS, Yuriy Mazur, Melkor3D, Outer Space, sdecoret)

Library of Congress Cataloging-in-Publication Data

Names: Karst, Ken, author.
Title: Alien abductions / Ken Karst.
Series: Enduring mysteries.
Includes bibliographical references and index.
Summary: An investigative approach to the curious phenomena and mysterious circumstances surrounding
alien abductions, from abductees' hypnotic recollections to conspiracy theories to hard facts.

Identifiers: LCCN 2017060031
ISBN 978-1-64026-005-4 (hardcover) / ISBN 978-1-62832-556-0 (pbk) / ISBN 978-1-64000-030-8 (eBook)
Subjects: LCSH: 1. Human-alien encounters—Juvenile literature. 2. Alien abduction—Juvenile literature. 3. Unidenti-
fied flying objects—Sightings and encounters.
Classification: LCC BF2050.K37 2018 / DDC 001.942—dc23

CCSS: RI.5.1, 2, 3, 6, 8; RH.6–8.4, 5, 6, 7, 8

First Edition HC   9 8 7 6 5 4 3 2 1
First Edition PBK   9 8 7 6 5 4 3 2 1

CREATIVE EDUCATION • CREATIVE PAPERBACKS

Table of Contents

Introduction   4

What Was *That*?   7
   Fake News, 1938   15
A Few Explanations   16
   Who Writes This Stuff?   25
The Abduction Hall of Fame   27
   Who You Gonna Call?   35
Plenty of Questions   36
   Campaigning ETs   45

Field Notes   46
Selected Bibliography   47
Websites   47
Index   48

Betty and Barney Hill set out for a weekend honeymoon in September 1961. What a honeymoon it was! Driving late at night from Montreal, Canada, back to their home in New Hampshire, the Hills spotted what they thought was an unusually bright star. But it was moving, and it was heading toward them. When they came to Franconia Notch, a pass in the White Mountains, they encountered some kind of large ship hovering over the road. They stopped the car and got out for a closer look. Barney could see figures in military uniforms through the aircraft's windows. "We have to get out of here, or we're going to be captured!" he hollered to Betty. They ran back to the car and quickly pulled away. Farther down the road, they felt a low buzzing sensation. At home, the couple noticed their watches had both broken at the same time. The car had polished circular spots on it. These strange spots made Betty's compass spin. Their drive had taken several hours longer than it should have. The Hills worked with researchers to piece together their experience. Their story was the first account of an alien abduction to gain international attention.

WHAT WAS *THAT?*

Our skies are filled with all manner of flying devices. Airplanes large and small zoom and putter over our heads. Helicopters hover above accidents or traffic jams and deliver sick and injured people to hospital rooftops. Weather balloons carrying packages of scientific instruments are launched simultaneously from dozens of sites across the United States every day. These balloons later fall to the ground. Satellites orbit Earth many miles above us, looking like slow but steadily moving stars.

There are some things moving through the skies that people can't recognize. These airborne crafts might have unusual lights. They might move in strange ways. They might hover, dart, or suddenly disappear. These are known as unidentified flying objects (UFOs). UFO sightings have steadily increased over the years, with most originating in the U.S. In 2017, a psychology doctoral student at Virginia's George Mason University reported that the number of sightings in the U.S. is 300 times the **median** for all countries. They're reported most frequently in the western and northwestern states.

The National UFO Reporting Center (NUFORC), which is not a government agency, lists sightings going back to **colonial** times. Until the Civil War (1861–65), entire decades sometimes passed without a report. Sightings increased during and after World War II (1939–45). The first year in which a UFO was reported every month was 1961. By 1999, monthly reports were numbering in the hundreds. The first month with more than 1,000 sightings was July 2014. The things people report as UFOs often turn out to be aircraft, lights, or even clouds. Some are sprites—massive electrical discharges that flare upward above storm clouds. Sprites tend to be shaped like jellyfish. They are usually reddish-orange near the top, with bluish **tendrils** hanging below. Even so, it's clear we are living in the UFO Age.

Seeing a UFO may be fairly common. But meeting the beings from

Glowing brightly in the dark sky, sprites might appear to be flying saucers rather than what they are—flashes of electrical energy.

inside the craft? That's a story that could make you a best-selling author. Or it could make your friends think you're a little weird. Or both.

Descriptions of such encounters typically have a lot in common. Often, people are in a car, traveling at night on a deserted country road. A UFO descends from the sky and stops in front of them. It's a large craft, usually with brightly colored lights. The driver and passengers feel overcome by peculiar forces. The vehicle's engine conks out. The people see strange figures emerge. The figures take the people out of their car and into the UFO. If the visitors arrive at a house or other building, they often enter by striding right through walls. They take people out the same way. The humans are unable to resist. It's as though they're paralyzed or half-asleep. The figures from the UFO are frequently described as small and grayish, with large heads and eyes. They make strange sounds with their mouths. Sometimes they manage to communicate with the people. The beings somehow put people at ease. Then they perform some kind of medical procedure on the people, often probing with needles. Then the UFO streaks out of sight. People report a period of time they can't remember.

Today, these events are known as alien abductions. Aliens are beings from somewhere other than Earth. (In legal terms, an "alien" means someone is from another country and isn't a citizen of the one in which he or she now lives.) Space aliens come from other planets or stars. An abduction is an event in which a person is unexpectedly forced to go somewhere without agreeing to be taken there. It's like a kidnapping.

Aliens in popular culture are commonly portrayed as having large eyes and elongated heads while flying in disk-shaped spacecraft known as "flying saucers."

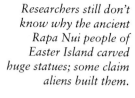

Researchers still don't know why the ancient Rapa Nui people of Easter Island carved huge statues; some claim aliens built them.

Aliens apparently aren't choosy about the people they abduct. They don't target religious leaders, elected officials, Olympic athletes, wealthy bankers, scholars, or pageant winners. Barney Hill was a postal worker. Betty Hill was a social worker. People who've been abducted include farmers, teachers, artists, housewives, and even law enforcement officers.

Some people who have been abducted, like author Whitley Strieber, say it has happened to them dozens of times for many years. Some, like Betty Hill, encourage their abductors to return for another meeting. Researchers say that if a person gets abducted once, they're likely to get abducted again. Another theory proposes that abductees had been **conceived** during alien encounters with their parents. That would make them half-alien and half-human. Future abductions could then be considered family reunions!

Many people believe aliens have been visiting Earth for thousands of years. Some say they came to mine gold. Others say aliens left behind valuable knowledge and skills. They believe the aliens helped design and build things that people long ago wouldn't have been able to make on their own. Did aliens direct the building of the pyramids? Did they carve and place almost a thousand 13-foot-tall (4 m) carved heads on Easter Island, off the coast of Chile? Did they hoist 25-ton (22.7 t) stones into a circle at England's Stonehenge? Did they draw and carve strange figures on rock walls?

More recently, people have wondered whether aliens have been capturing people for scientific studies. Betty Hill said her captors sank a long needle into her navel. She thought this was an effort to see if she was pregnant. Researchers have noted that her description was similar to a procedure called **amniocentesis**. But when Betty was abducted, amniocentesis was just being developed. Her captors seemed to have an advanced understanding of it.

Several researchers and writers, such as Budd Hopkins and David M. Jacobs, claim that aliens are abducting humans and using them to create a new hybrid species. Hopkins wrote that aliens are forcing abductees to mate with one another in situations they control or are taking human eggs to develop elsewhere. "All of the evidence points to their being here to carry out a complex breeding experiment," Hopkins wrote in his 1996 book *Witnessed*. He added that alien abductions have been used to reunite parents with their human-alien offspring.

Some believe that in the late 1940s, the U.S. government and aliens made an agreement. Aliens would be allowed to land on Earth and harvest human organs because their own were failing. In exchange, the aliens would provide advanced research into the technologies that enabled them to fly to Earth. Jacobs, who is the founder and director of the International Center

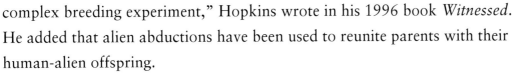

for Abduction Research (ICAR), noted that aliens probably wouldn't need a contract to operate on Earth.

A 2015 YouGov.com poll calculated that 30 percent of Americans believed the government was covering up evidence of visits by aliens. A poll for a British talk show in 2014 determined that 1 in 25 people believed he or she had been abducted by aliens.

But alien abductions have to compete for attention with frightening earthbound events. Chris Carter created *The X-Files*, a popular television series based on alien contacts. He has said that the 9/11 terrorist attacks and destruction of the World Trade Center in 2001 overshadowed interest in **extraterrestrials**. Fear is now inspired more by terrorists—especially people with bombs—than by the thought of aliens. The Intruders Foundation, established by Hopkins in 1989 to offer support to people who had been abducted by aliens, disbanded in 2011 after Hopkins died. These days, people are more likely to think of computer **hackers** than aliens when technology goes haywire.

Fake News, 1938 On a Sunday evening in October 1938, millions of Americans tuned their radios to a comedy routine on NBC. After the short bit ended, many flipped over to CBS. There they heard an alarming report that a meteor had crashed into a field in New Jersey. That was followed by a frantic reporter's description of the scene. It wasn't a meteor. It was a Martian attack! The Martians were too frightening to look at, he said. Soon they had wiped out 7,000 National Guardsmen and released poisonous gas. Many people had missed the CBS introduction, which described the report as a radio play. Shortly, New Jersey highways were jammed with people trying to escape. Telephone lines crashed, people demanded gas masks from police, and some tried to get power companies to turn off lights so that the Martians couldn't see where people lived. The creator of the show, Orson Welles, went back on the air to explain that it was fiction. It was a new dramatic version of the 19th-century science fiction novel *War of the Worlds*. The panic subsided. No one was killed or abducted. Welles, only 23 at the time, went on to become one of America's greatest actors and filmmakers.

A FEW
EXPLANATIONS

In 1947, some kind of aircraft crashed near Roswell, New Mexico. A rancher came across the debris and called the sheriff, who in turn called a nearby army base. An officer on duty put out a statement describing the thing that had crashed as a "flying disk."

A *what*? It was only two years after atomic bombs had been detonated over Japan, ending World War II. The war had produced numerous advances in technology. Some, like nuclear weapons, were both incredible and frightening. Now flying saucers from Mars, or wherever, were crash-landing on U.S. soil? The news roared across the nation, but only briefly. The very next day, the army offered another story. It had only been a weather balloon, with metal reflectors.

The weather balloon story had its day in the press. Some yawned. Others said: Not so fast! A story that changes so completely and so quickly is almost always suspicious. Indeed, seven decades later, many people still believe the government lied about what happened at Roswell. They continue to believe that aliens were recovered alive from the wreckage and were used by the government for research. The Roswell incident coincided with the dawn of the Cold War. That was a period after World War II when the Soviet Union and the U.S. (and each side's allies) were struggling for power. Spying and secrecy were the chief weapons employed in the conflict. Then, in 1957, the Soviet Union launched *Sputnik*, the first artificial satellite. Space travel and space spying were suddenly possible. The launch energized people's faith in technology, as well as their curiosity, suspicion, and fears about the unknown. With *Sputnik* circling the globe, the Roswell alien spacecraft story

Following the Roswell incident and the launch of Sputnik, *many people became convinced the U.S. government knew more about aliens than it was letting on.*

expanded in many directions. Reports of UFO sightings multiplied dramatically. And those led to reports of encounters with alien creatures—which turned into reports of abductions.

The story of Betty and Barney Hill became public in 1965, four years after their reported abduction experience. About the same time, a story emerged about a Brazilian farmer, Antônio Villas Boas, who claimed to have been abducted in 1957 while plowing a field at night.

Numerous abduction stories followed, mostly in the U.S. They shared many similarities with acts occurring before, during, and after the abductions. The aliens often paralyzed the humans or coaxed people to follow them to their ship. They used some form of reassuring communication, even though they didn't make any recognizable sounds. Sometimes they didn't make any sound at all. After performing a sort of medical examination, the aliens let the people go. In the days and weeks that followed, the people frequently had nightmares or other anxieties. They also suffered from headaches and other illnesses. Many went to **psychiatrists**. They were sometimes put under **hypnosis** to try to recall and describe their abductions.

Abductees, who are also called "experiencers," might be reluctant to talk about their encounters. They think people won't believe them. Abductees often talk about how the aliens walked through the walls of their home, and then took them out the same way. That sort of thing seems impossible to most people. But experiencers are convinced it happened to them. They say the aliens even have names. Betty Andreasson, abducted from her Massachusetts home in a famous 1967 incident, knew that the leader of the group that abducted her was called Quazgaa.

Experiencers are not necessarily religious people. They don't typically

Rumors of an alien spaceship crashing in Roswell, New Mexico, sparked a flurry of UFO sightings and reports of alien encounters.

believe the aliens came from heaven. Nor do they claim their abductors were sent by God. The aliens don't perform miracles. Few encounters involve meeting people who have died on Earth and gone elsewhere.

Andreasson is a strongly religious person. She prayed often during her encounter. She said that at one point, confronted by a huge, eagle-like bird, she felt that God was speaking to her. But she has also said that, while her abduction wasn't a religious experience, it was made possible by her spirituality. Andreasson was an artist and drew dozens of detailed pictures of her abduction. Many of them are included in a book titled *The Andreasson Affair*. Most of the works resemble technical drawings or illustrations. None of the figures has wings or halos, like angels. None shows figures rising into the sky.

There are numerous organizations that collect and analyze reports about UFOs and alien abductions. The best-known is probably the Mutual

UFO Network (MUFON). Another is Jacobs's ICAR. Some psychiatrists also offer support groups in which experiencers can compare their insights. But Jacobs notes that acceptance is hard to find, both from scholars and from the folks next door. "The majority of evidence for the alien abduction **phenomenon** is from human memory derived from hypnosis administered by amateurs," Jacobs writes. "It is difficult to imagine a weaker form of evidence.... Abduction researchers are mainly amateurs doing their best to get to the truth, knowing that objective reality may elude them."

Indeed, there is a large body of research, much of it performed by psychiatrists, saying that alien encounters don't really happen. They're imaginary. The people who say that are known as "skeptics." Many of them publish articles in a magazine called *Skeptical Inquirer*.

One of the most common criticisms is directed at the role of hypnotism, exactly as Jacobs has suggested. Experiencers often go to psychiatrists after their abductions to try to better understand what happened. The psychiatrist will sometimes hypnotize the patient and ask for details. Stories recalled under hypnosis have been classified as "inherently unreliable" by the California Supreme Court.

Skeptics insist that abductees' encounters with aliens are imagined; people's thoughts and memories can easily be influenced by what they have seen elsewhere.

Numerous researchers say the people doing the hypnotizing can guide the patient to say whatever the hypnotizer wants or to "remember" things that never happened. Even without hypnosis, people have confessed to murders that they didn't commit. That suggests that the human mind can be fooled.

Skeptics say that, just because abduction stories share many components, it doesn't make them accurate. They could be similar because experiencers have absorbed details from others' stories and pictures. Many experiencers had in fact heard or read about abductions in the weeks leading up to their own experience. Some say the popularity of alien abduction stories in science fiction, comic books, on television, and in movies is one reason why aliens almost always have big heads and big, almond-shaped eyes. Because of these popular media portrayals, people already know what aliens "look" like before they are abducted! As for why experiencers often describe a sort of paralysis when the aliens arrive, that's easy to explain, too. We often have that feeling at the onset of sleep or just upon waking.

Being able to describe an alien abduction doesn't mean you're crazy, some psychiatrists note. They call it "fantasy prone." Perhaps your parents convinced you one of your dolls could understand you. You may now have trouble distinguishing fantasy from reality. You're more likely to have **hallucinations**. And, coincidentally, you're easy to hypnotize.

Famed skeptic Robert A. Baker, a professor emeritus of psychology at the University of Kentucky, summed up alien abductions this way: "What we have learned about aliens thus far tells us only one thing: they're not alien at all, they're human."

Who Writes This Stuff?

Three of the best-known writers about alien abductions have brought a high level of accomplishment in other fields to their work. John E. Mack was a psychiatry professor at Harvard University Medical School who also won a Pulitzer Prize. He studied experiencers, estimating there were one million of them in the U.S. Mack was heavily criticized by some fellow scholars for researching abductions. He died in 2004 at age 74. David M. Jacobs is a retired Temple University history professor who taught what is believed to have been the nation's only college course on UFOs. He founded ICAR. He has written several books about abductions and UFOs. Jacobs stands behind the idea that alien abductors are here to breed with humans. That links him with Budd Hopkins (pictured), perhaps the most popular author and researcher into abductions. Until he was about 50, Hopkins was best known as an artist. His paintings and sculptures are in the permanent collections of some major museums. But he then wrote several books on alien abductions, based on interviews with experiencers. One was turned into a 1992 television miniseries, *Intruders*. Hopkins died in 2011 at age 80.

THE ABDUCTION HALL OF FAME

Getting abducted by aliens doesn't guarantee you'll become famous. It does promise that people will ask you a lot of questions. On the other hand, some may decide they don't want you talking to their kids anymore. There are so many alien abduction stories that yours had better be good in order to stand out. Here are some you'd be competing with:

Betty and Barney Hill did not need to call more attention to themselves. For one thing, Betty was white, and Barney was black. In the early 1960s, interracial couples were extremely rare in the U.S. After their 1961 abduction on a deserted mountain road in New Hampshire, the Hills had many health problems and were plagued by nightmares. A mysterious circle of warts emerged on Barney's leg. They tried to go about their normal lives. Barney continued to be active in civil rights causes and was appointed to government advisory positions. They did not want to make their story public. But they told it to groups in their Unitarian church and worked with several psychiatrists and researchers. A Boston newspaper broke the story several years later. That led to a best-selling book, *Interrupted Journey*, in 1966. *The UFO Incident*, a made-for-TV movie starring James Earl Jones, followed in 1975. Many strange things continued to happen in their home. Barney died in 1969. Betty, whose sister had been abducted separately, continued to see UFOs and have other odd experiences. She later became an advocate for experiencers. But she had so many stories that many people stopped believing her. Betty Hill died in 2004.

Betty Andreasson was abducted from her kitchen in Massachusetts in 1967. She said a group of four small, gray aliens seeped right through the walls of her house, while their ship glowed in the backyard. Her parents and seven children, in the next room, were somehow immobilized. One daughter

Barney and Betty Hill reportedly saw a strange light as they were driving, and when they got out of the car to investigate, they were allegedly abducted.

witnessed and recalled the encounter. The aliens implanted some kind of device into Andreasson's nose. They took a sample from her navel. They also made duplicate copies of her Bible. Andreasson and her husband eventually divorced. She later married a man who was also an experiencer. They had many **paranormal** experiences, such as out-of-body episodes, UFO sightings, and periods of missing time. Like the Hills, Betty Andreasson underwent hypnosis to recall her experiences. Her daughter did as well and recounted numerous abductions.

Linda Napolitano's 1989 abduction could have been a crowd favorite, since it happened near the Brooklyn Bridge in New York City. Author Budd Hopkins asserted in *Witnessed* that hers is the only alien abduction ever seen by other people who weren't abducted in the same incident. In the book, Hopkins called Napolitano "Linda Cortile." Clad in a nightgown, Napolitano was floated out the window of her 12th-floor apartment and taken into a hovering ship. The ship then plunged into the East River and did not reappear. Among the witnesses were a world political leader and his two drivers. Hopkins did not name the political figure other than to call him "the third man." Later reports asserted it was Javier Pérez de Cuéllar, then secretary-general of the United Nations. But neither Napolitano's abduction from the heart of New York City nor Pérez de Cuéllar's rumored witnessing of it was ever reported as a news story.

Whitley Strieber was nervous about break-ins at his family's cabin in upstate New York. He even installed a security system. So he was quite surprised one night in 1985 to see a figure standing by his bed. The next thing he knew, he was sitting outside in the woods. After some hypnosis, Strieber came to believe he had been abducted by aliens. The aliens subject-

Many experiencers say they saw a bright light and were pulled upward through the air into a waiting alien spacecraft.

ed him to medical tests. They inserted needles into his brain and rectum and took blood samples from his finger. Strieber, who had written several successful horror novels in the years prior, wrote an account of his abduction in *Communion*. He regarded it as nonfiction. Some critics have questioned similarities between that work and some of his earlier novels. Strieber said he likely developed those fictional characters based on repressed experiences with aliens. In later books, he wrote about encounters both before and since the incident at the cabin. They deal with the possibilities of time travel and **parallel universes**. Strieber maintains an online journal called Unknown Country.

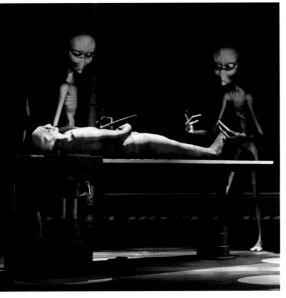

Arizona logger Travis Walton was driving home with some coworkers on November 5, 1975. A large, glowing disk appeared and hovered near them. Walton was curious. He jumped out of the truck and approached it. That's when a beam of light knocked him unconscious. His friends were so frightened they drove away. When they came back to get him, Walton was gone. Five days later, he was found on a road 12 miles (19.3 km) away from where he'd been hit by the light. Walton said he remembered awakening in a sort of exam room. Three short, humanoid aliens were working with him. After a while, a more human-like creature escorted him through a large building like an airplane hangar and helped him escape. Walton was abducted only two weeks after *The UFO Incident* aired on television. Some say that show probably planted the idea of an abduction in Walton's imagination. Walton's book about his encounter, *The Walton Experience*, led to the 1993 film, *Fire in the Sky*.

The film Fire in the Sky *(opposite) is based on Travis Walton's abduction account, in which space creatures experimented on him before setting him free.*

Countless other abduction reports have not been made into best-selling books or movies. But they illustrate the phenomenon all the same:

Two counselors at a camp along the shores of Lake Champlain in Burlington, Vermont, were on a dock one evening in August 1968. Their fellow counselors and the campers had gone into town for the day. The two noticed a bright light falling in the southwest. It seemed to come from the Adirondack Mountains across the lake. It came closer and appeared cigar-shaped. Then smaller lights emerged from it, turning into disks. One of them, like the craft that abducted Linda Napolitano, plummeted into the water. It created a large disturbance in the lake, and then emerged at the end of the dock. It shone a bright light on the counselors. The next thing they knew, they were back on the dock and heard car doors slamming as everyone else returned. At least one of the returnees saw the UFO departing. Under hypnosis, the two counselors who had been on the dock recalled floating on a beam of light into the UFO. They were examined by four small, greenish-blue occupants with large heads and large, protruding eyes. One of them described seeing Earth through a window of the UFO as if it were in distant space.

Four men canoeing through the Allagash Wilderness Waterway in northern Maine in 1976 were briefly enveloped in a cone of light from a craft hovering above them. Then the craft sped away. Years later, the men started having nightmares about that night. Under hypnosis, they separately recalled being pulled up through the cone of light into the UFO. There they were examined by three or four occupants. Then they were returned to the canoe. The men had been students together at the Massachusetts College of Art and Design. One of them drew a detailed series of sketches of the aliens.

Who You Gonna Call?

The best-known organization for investigating alien abductions is MUFON. It was founded in Illinois in 1969 and now has an estimated 4,000 members around the world. Most of them are in the U.S. The organization deals with many aspects of UFO sightings. Its mission is to investigate UFOs to "discover the true nature of the phenomenon, with an eye towards scientific breakthroughs and improving life on our planet." At its annual meeting, MUFON offers special sessions for experiencers. It has an entire team of people to work with experiencers. One of MUFON's directors is Kathleen Marden, a niece of Betty and Barney Hill's. She has written several books on abductions. She helps experiencers work with ways to resist or even end their abductions. The group also has a broad network of investigators. Investigators are expected to have strong interviewing skills. They should understand that some UFO reports are not mysteries. Some UFOs are really just odd weather occurrences or aircraft. Investigators are encouraged to understand astronomy. They should be handy with photographic equipment and methods. They're expected to help people reporting UFOs remain anonymous, or unnamed. MUFON is active on Twitter and Facebook.

PLENTY OF QUESTIONS

Earth is believed to be about 4.5 billion years old. The earliest relatives of humans appeared only about 3 million years ago. Scientists suggest that the humans we might recognize today developed about 200,000 years ago. Now, let's convert those time periods into manageable chunks: If life on Earth began 1 year ago, humans would have first appeared about 23 minutes ago. In other words, we're newcomers.

That raises a lot of questions about aliens and alien abductions. Betty and Barney Hill came to believe they were abducted by aliens from Zeta Reticuli, a pair of stars. Zeta Reticuli is 39 light years away. That means it would take 39 years for something moving at the speed of light to travel that distance. Light travels at a rate of about 186,282 miles (299,792 km) per second. One light year is nearly 6 trillion miles. Light can travel that fast because it has no mass. A spaceship with several human-like creatures aboard (even if they were small), and equipped with medical testing devices, furniture, and supplies would move much more slowly. So if aliens came to Earth from Zeta Reticuli, it would have taken a very long time. They'd probably be really old! (Of course, aliens might age at different rates from humans.) Why would both aliens and human have emerged, developed, and survived on different planets at apparently the same pace and the same time? Why aren't we as advanced as aliens? Because our species hasn't been on the planet very long, there would

have to be a lot of luck involved in aliens meeting us at all.

Why do aliens keep coming? Why don't they show any interest in plants or animals that might provide food on some distant star? Why would they come for gold, and not for oxygen, or hydrogen, or other **elements** they might use to sustain life or create energy? Why would they repeatedly return for human samples? It seems like an awfully long trip just for some medical tests. And that leads to another big question: Why don't they just take humans back with them? There are very few accounts of people being taken to other worlds. If, as some researchers suggest, aliens are creating an alien-human species, they might be doing it elsewhere. Those hybrid creatures might be living in other galaxies far, far away.

How have aliens found us? Earth is a small planet circling a star that is one of billions in our galaxy. And our galaxy is among perhaps 200 billion. We emit radio signals into space from many of our daily activities. But that's been happening for a little more than 100 years. Those signals travel at the

Researchers note that experimental disk-shaped aircraft have proven to be unstable and inefficient, with difficulties achieving liftoff from the ground.

A British engineer developed a saucer-shaped hovercraft in the 1950s; the vehicle could travel over water as well as land.

speed of light, but they weaken with distance. It's unlikely that aliens on Zeta Reticuli could detect a signal from Earth. Even if they could, it would have been about 1940 before any signal reached them. If they hopped immediately into something that could somehow transport them at the speed of light, they still would not have gotten to Earth until about 1980. The aliens who abducted Betty and Barney Hill did so well before then. They had to know about Earth some other way. How? Or did they find our tiny planet by accident?

Despite our technological advances, humans appear to be far behind when it comes to discovering other worlds. We've managed only to land some scientific instruments on planets nearby. We certainly have not traveled to other solar systems or galaxies. Our own attempt at a flying saucer, paid for by the U.S. government, couldn't get more than three feet (0.9 m)

off the ground before crashing in 1961. Why would aliens want to understand us, since we've accomplished so little in comparison?

Our inability to visit other stars and their planets means we have not abducted any aliens ourselves. Many people believe that the craft that crashed near Roswell, New Mexico, in 1947 had aliens aboard. Supposedly, the military and research workers took those aliens to Area 51, a military base in Nevada where secret experiments have been carried out for many years. But did anyone take samples? Did anyone learn anything from the aliens? Were they bred with humans? No one's ever said.

So are we alone in the universe, without even alien neighbors? A long-running project aims to learn just that. The Search for Extraterrestrial Intelligence (SETI) has been underway since the development of radio signals. It is now coordinated by the SETI Institute in California. It involves all kinds of radio signal–detectors around the world and even includes individ-

Some conspiracy theorists believe the U.S. government secretly studies alien spacecraft that have crash-landed on Earth.

uals using home computers. In 1977, a SETI researcher at Ohio State University picked up a strong signal with a radio telescope. It lasted 72 seconds. Many scientists believed it could have been a signal from some intelligent life form and activity elsewhere in the universe. Scientists got so excited they called it the "Wow!" signal. But the original signal has never been detected again. SETI researchers are trying to sort out reports of a signal detected in Russia in 2015 that might have come from a planet 94 light years away. The chances are small. Regardless, scientists are still operating with the understanding that there could very well be other forms of life out there. Some, including the renowned physicist Stephen Hawking, have cautioned that humans should be wary when making contact with alien beings. Of course, aliens who've abducted humans have done so gently, according to experiencers. Nations have developed global rules for the treatment of prisoners. But there are no such rules for alien abductions. Scientists and others around the world are trying to agree on what kind of message humans might prepare to send aliens. The idea is to avoid a misunderstanding or even a conflict.

Recent studies suggest that the "Wow!" signal received by SETI was triggered by what was, at the time, an as-yet unidentified comet.

Meanwhile, humans haven't had any difficulty imagining what abductions or other encounters with aliens might be like. Numerous popular science fiction books have dealt with alien meetings. Films from as long ago as *A Trip to the Moon* in 1902 to *Independence Day* in 1996 and its 2016 sequel, *Independence Day: Resurgence*, have revolved around encounters with aliens—not all of them pleasant. In the 1951 film *The Day the Earth Stood Still*, aliens landed on the White

House lawn to warn humans that the rest of the galaxy would destroy Earth if its residents continued to make war and use nuclear bombs. *E.T. the Extra-Terrestrial* (1982) involved a sweet and sometimes comic alien abduction. However, the "abduction" was in reverse, since the extraterrestrial was left behind on Earth and protected by a young boy. Television's *Saturday Night Live* made landmark comedy about the idea of aliens living among us, in the "Coneheads" skits. And *Mork and Mindy*, a comedy starring Robin Williams, featured an alien who came not to abduct humans but to live among them, learn their customs, and report back to his home planet of Ork.

Alien abductions, both as entertainment and as reports to police and psychiatrists, are likely to continue for quite some time. Humans have always been interested in whether there are other beings in the universe. Space exploration and communication technologies are bringing us closer to whatever might be out there. We might feel small and insignificant in the universe. But when someone, or something, travels millions of miles to visit and learn from us, it makes us feel important.

The secrets of outer space and the possibility of finding life on other planets continue to intrigue people of all ages.

Campaigning ETs Candidates for U.S. president try to appeal to many different voters, but extraterrestrials? Their status got a boost in the 2016 election campaign from Democratic nominee Hillary Clinton. Asked by a reporter for a New Hampshire newspaper whether Earth has been visited by extraterrestrials, Clinton said, "I think we may have been....We don't know for sure." Clinton said if she became president, she would make public whatever the government knows about aliens and their visits, as long as it did not harm national security. Her position encouraged many people who have long believed the government has covered up information about possible encounters with aliens. "There's enough stories out there that I don't think everybody is just sitting in their kitchen making them up," she said in another interview. It's long been reported that Clinton has an interest in paranormal communications. She was ridiculed for it when her husband, Bill, was president. In 1993, a tabloid published a story that she had adopted an alien baby. In any case, she showed some expertise on the subject during the 2016 campaign when she corrected a talk show host on his use of the term "UFO." "It's unexplained aerial phenomenon," she said. "UAP. That's the latest nomenclature [term]."

Field Notes

amniocentesis: a surgical process in which fluid is removed by needle from a pregnant woman's uterus and used to diagnose the condition of the fetus

colonial: the period in American history before 1776, when the nation that would become the U.S. was ruled by England

conceived: given life, or became pregnant

elements: substances that cannot be broken down into simpler components

extraterrestrials: beings from beyond Earth

hackers: people who break through computer program protections and steal information or alter how specific computers or networks operate

hallucinations: physical perceptions of things that do not exist outside the mind

hypnosis: a highly suggestive mental state, usually induced by a psychiatrist, used to help a person recall experiences, deal with pain, or change behavior

median: the middle value, with half above and half below

parallel universes: realities that coexist with one's own

paranormal: outside what can be understood by science

phenomenon: an occurrence that can be observed

psychiatrists: doctors who diagnose and treat mental illnesses

tendrils: thin, threadlike extensions of a plant or animal

Selected Bibliography

A&E Networks. *The Young Investigator's Guide to Ancient Aliens*. New York: Roaring Brook, 2015.

Fowler, Raymond E. *The Andreasson Affair: The True Story of a Close Encounter of the Fourth Kind*. Pompton Plains, N.J.: Career Press, 2015.

Frazier, Kendrick, Barry Karr, and Joe Nickell, eds. *The UFO Invasion: The Roswell Incident, Alien Abductions, and Government Coverups*. Amherst, N.Y.: Prometheus Books, 1997.

Gallagher, Danny. *The Six Most Famous Alien Abductions*. The FW. http://thefw.com/famous-alien-abductions/.

Hopkins, Budd. *Witnessed: The True Story of the Brooklyn Bridge UFO Abductions*. New York: Pocket Books, 1996.

Marden, Kathleen, and Stanton Friedman. *Captured! The Betty and Barney Hill UFO Experience: The True Story of the World's First Documented Alien Abduction*. Franklin Lakes, N.J.: New Page Books, 2007.

Websites

ALIEN ABDUCTION EXPERIENCE AND RESEARCH
http://www.abduct.com/

THE CONVERSATION: SOME SCIENTIFIC EXPLANATIONS FOR ALIEN ABDUCTION THAT AREN'T SO OUT OF THIS WORLD
http://www.abduct.com/

Note: Every effort has been made to ensure that any websites listed above were active at the time of publication. However, because of the nature of the Internet, it is impossible to guarantee that these sites will remain active indefinitely or that their contents will not be altered.

Index

A

abductions 4–5, 11, 12, 13, 14,
  20, 22–23, 25, 28, 31–32,
  34, 35, 28, 40
  Antônio Villas Boas 20
  Barney and Betty Hill 4–5,
    12, 13, 20, 28, 31, 35,
    38, 40
  Betty Andreasson 20, 22, 28,
    31
  Linda Napolitano 31, 34
  Travis Walton 32
  Whitley Strieber 12, 31–32
aircraft 8, 9, 19, 35
Area 51 41

C

Civil War 9
Clinton, Hillary 45
Cold War 19
cultural portrayals 14, 15, 22,
  24, 25, 28, 31–32, 43–44
  films and television 14, 24,
    25, 28, 32, 43–44
  literature 15, 22, 24, 25, 28,
    31, 32
  radio programs 15

E

Easter Island 12

H

hypnosis 20, 23–24, 31, 32, 34

P

psychiatrists 20, 23, 24, 25,
  28, 44
pyramids 12

R

research organizations 9,
  13–14, 22–23, 25, 35, 41,
  43
  International Center for Ab-
    duction Research (ICAR)
    13–14, 23, 25
  Intruders Foundation 14
  Mutual UFO Network
    (MUFON) 22, 23, 35
  National UFO Reporting
    Center (NUFORC) 9
  Search for Extraterrestrial
    Intelligence (SETI) 41, 43
researchers 13–14, 22–23, 25,
  31
  Budd Hopkins 13, 14, 25, 31
  David M. Jacobs 13–14, 23,
    25
  John E. Mack 25
Roswell, New Mexico 19–20,
  41

S

satellites 8, 19
skeptics 23, 24
  Robert A. Baker 24
Soviet Union 19
Stonehenge 12

T

terrorism 14

U

UFOs 4, 8–9, 11, 19, 20, 23,
  25, 28, 31, 32, 34, 35, 38,
  40, 41, 45
  reported sightings 8–9, 19, 20,
    23, 28, 31, 32, 34, 35

U.S. government 13, 14, 19,
  40, 45

W

weather 9, 35
  clouds 9
  sprites 9
weather balloons 8, 19
World War II 9, 19

Z

Zeta Reticuli 38, 40